HOW TO PRESENT
BUSINESS
OPPORTUNITY

STEP BY STEP FROM NEWBIES TO PROFESSIONAL

SAI JAMES

How to present business opportunity

Step By Step

from Newbies to Professional

Introduction

How to present business opportunity Step By Step from Newbies to Professional is a book that will give you a simple and easy rundown of how best to present your business to all sorts of people. It doesn't matter if you are new to network marketing or if you've done it for years. This book will surely have some informational tidbits that you can use in your networking and multi-level marketing strategy.

In this book, you will find easy to follow tips and steps that will help you in presenting the business opportunities you offer, from building up your self-confidence, to making an extensive clients list, to making invitations and getting commitments from your prospects. These tips and steps will help you become a more effective network marketer and team leader, as well as give you insights on some subtle and not-so-subtle errors that a lot of marketers tend to make.

Thank you for downloading this book. I hope you enjoy reading it!

Chapter 1: Multi-Level Marketing and Network Marketing Basics

When you start out as a new company, getting the word out about your product, service, or methods can be very expensive. Before MLM and Network Marketing, companies would have to hire big ad agencies or employ a big sales team to effectively spread the word, but these options are always so expensive and hardly practical for start-up companies.

Fortunately, there is an alternative route that's been steadily gaining ground and popularity—Network Marketing and Multi-Level Marketing. Through these marketing styles, small start-up companies can get the word out there without having to pay huge sums to big advertising companies. Instead, all that money can be spent to pay distributors and agents who advertise through word-of-mouth. This will allow business owners to grow their business without having to take the typical risks that come with it. But for you to be able to make good use of these marketing strategies, you should first have an understanding of all the basics when it comes to network marketing and multi-level marketing.

Network Marketing or Direct Sales

This business model is one that has found a way to get out of hiring the middlemen. This means that companies are directly marketing to the consumers through independent distributors. With this business model, companies can save a lot of money on advertising and hiring a big sales team, and companies can then use the savings as rewards for the distributors, in the form of commissions and bonuses.

This means that the company no longer spends huge amounts of money on advertising tricks that may or may not pay off, the distributor earns extra by recommending a product they believe in and has most likely even tested, and the consumer will buy a product that they know has value and was recommended to them rather than falling for a spiffy online or print ad or an amusing TV commercial. Everybody wins in this scenario. Simple, isn't it?

Multi-Level Marketing

Multi-level Marketing can seem very complicated, and at some point it really is. Multi-level marketing is like network marketing doubled many times over. Instead of straightforward direct sales by the distributor, independent distributors are encouraged to recruit more people as their sales force, training them to become leaders in their own right.

Members of your sales force are, in turn, encouraged to recruit other independent distributors and become leaders of their own teams. All those you recruited, as well as their succeeding recruits, will fall under your "business umbrella." In MLM terms, they become part of your downline and are placed beneath you on the business chart. This downline consists of many levels, which is why it is called the multi-level marketing model. Whatever profits are earned by those in your downline, even if they were never directly contacted by you but only by those under you, can mean profits for you as well.

So basically, the benefits that can be gained from network marketing still stand when it comes to ML marketing, but the rewards you reap as you get more independent distributors on board become greater.

With network marketing and ML marketing, a lot of money can be saved, a big part of which then finds its way to the distributor's pockets. It's a great way for small businesses to start out and for marketing newbies and professionals to earn some extra cash. These networking techniques have changed the lives of countless people, and it's about time you get a slice of the pie.

But remember, it's never wise to lose steam early on. Business is a roller coaster ride: sometimes you're going up and sometimes you're going down. However, if you manage to develop the proper technique and skills you can find in this book, you can expect the profits to start rolling in.

Chapter 2: Starting Out, from Confidence, to list Building

Starting out in Network marketing and ML marketing can be a little scary for the untrained newbie, and a lot of marketing professionals can fall into a funk, too. Network marketers with some years behind them can find their sales going down and it's always a good idea to refresh some of your methods or even try to change your tactics. This chapter will mostly deal with what you need to do and develop before you go out and start your network and multi-level marketing strategy.

Have Full Confidence in the Company, the Profession, and Yourself

Before you can start selling your product and convincing others to sell it too, you have to be sold on it yourself. This means that you can guarantee the product or service, the company, and the benefits without any doubt. There are certainly some businesses out there with questionable intentions that have made use of these legitimate business models to earn quick profits, but the façade breaks down rather quickly once the weak points show.

Legitimate businesses, on the other hand, have proven time and again how profitable the business model is, and companies, distributors, as well as the consumers have greatly benefitted from this. You must not doubt the legitimacy of your profession despite being faced with the uninformed views and opinions of certain individuals, which you will encounter eventually (if you haven't already). In the same sense, the products, compensation plans, and services offered by established network marketing companies have also been proven through time, as well as by you and by those in your upline i.e. the ones above you in the business chart.

If the company you are working with is relatively new, you have to make sure that it promotes a product or a service that you know truly delivers. You have to truly believe in it and have basic knowledge of the ins and outs of the company. Direct marketing and Multi-level marketing is based on trust and rapport between the team leader, their teams, and the consumer, and those relationships based on deception will never last or benefit anybody in the end.

Lastly, you have to have belief in yourself. Without belief in yourself, you cannot sell even the best product from the most reliable and most well-known company. Being uncertain and timid when it comes to selling your product will make the consumers doubt not only you, but the product and company as well. If even you seem uncertain about a product, how can you expect others to buy into it as well? It is important that you develop confidence in yourself for you to be able to convince other people.

Tip: *For building up self-confidence on the field*

If you find yourself faltering when you start your pitch, or even when you're just on the phone, you can try practicing what you have to say to a friend or a family member. You can even just practice what you are going to say in front of a mirror. Work on your delivery and try to sound as confident as you can. Keep at it until you've memorized the words and deliver them with ease. You won't get it perfect the first time, but keep practicing and improving your delivery and methods as you train yourself on the job.

Get out there as much as you can, and talk to as many people as possible

One of the things that can make you lose steam early on in your network marketing endeavor is pinning your hopes on a few people you know. This is actually a very normal response for most people, but it can end in disappointment. Network marketing and ML marketing rely on you finding enough clients or more distributors, and pinning your hopes on a small client base can cause you to lose steam early on.

Tip: *Start with a big list and keep adding to it*

Instead of making a small mental list of people you know, make an extensive list of <u>everyone</u> you know. It doesn't matter if you aren't very close or haven't been in contact with them for a while; just include them in your list of prospects. If you have a small list of 10 people, crossing out two or three can be a huge downer on your confidence and enthusiasm. On the other hand, starting with an extensive list of around 500 and crossing out a couple won't zap you right away; it can also open your eyes to the possibilities and prospects before you.

Also, don't limit your prospects only to the people you know. Keep adding to the list by imagining all the other people that your current prospects may have around them. If you have your parents on the list, then think of all their friends and acquaintances, and it's the same with your uncle, your college, and high school friends, etc. The longer the list gets, the more prospects you have and the bigger your odds of convincing more and more people.

Chapter 3: The Skills You'll Need When Handling Prospects

Once you have your confidence boosted, spent enough time practicing, and have your prospect list ready, it should be time to go out there and start going to face-to-face meetings or making your calls to your prospects. But how can you go about it successfully?

Be a Builder, not a Hunter

As mentioned earlier, network marketing and MLM thrive on personal experience and building up great relationships with your teams, other distributors, and the consumer. Your prospects have to feel comfortable and confident in the relationship you are building with them. Successful network marketers are builders and growers. They tend to their garden of prospects and shower it with trust and friendship so that it grows and blooms. They build up their relationships from acquaintances to true friendships. Instead of making a sale, they want to inform and educate their prospects. In doing so, they also build up their reputations and influence. In this way, their network and list of prospects never dwindle down but continue to grow.

There are others, however, who go about it as hunters. They track down their prospects and go for the kill, or the sale, in other words. Sometimes, they catch their prey, but most of the time, the prey gets away. This way of going about it can only end in failure. If you go about it thinking only of making the sale rather than developing a real relationship with your prospect, then they will feel cornered and be less likely to keep in touch or go into business with you. And the people you will manage to convince to join your business are going to end up copying the hunter style as well, which can end up with them getting disappointed with the results and quitting.

Remember that building good relationships with your prospects will eventually pay off. Some of them may say no for now, but the right time can come in a few years, months, or even just days. They may even have other prospects they can recommend to you. Do your best to continue to stay in touch with all your prospects. It doesn't always have to be about business; find creative ways to check in on them and make sure that your relationship doesn't die out. It will all pay off in the end.

Be engaging

When talking to your prospects, you can't just jump into your pitch right away. Remember to make your invitations appropriate. If you aren't right in your timing, you can end up annoying or turning off people, and you have to teach your team the same thing. You have to find ways to catch their attention and keep it, but in a more subtle way.

Be yourself. Don't turn into someone else once you start your pitch. This can make people feel suspicious and uncomfortable. Don't try to act the way you think a proper marketer ought to. It may sound cliché, but just be yourself, or at least, the best version of yourself that you can be. After all, your prospects should want to work with YOU, not the stranger that you become when you start inviting and making your pitch.

Display passion. Show others that you are passionate about what you do. Bring some positivity and cheerfulness to the table when communicating with new prospects. Such positive attitudes can be contagious and bring about a more positive outcome as well.

Exude confidence. You have to be confident, not just in your words and speech, but in your body language and posture as well. You have to have the bearing of someone who is worth listening to. Don't be apologetic when you ask for people's attention—be bold. Why should you apologize when you know that you are not wasting their time and that what you are saying will greatly benefit them in the end? Do your best to step out of your shell. Having confidence in yourself will influence prospects to have confidence in you.

The most successful networking marketers are the ones who have not been trying to just sell their products, but instead have developed human connections with their prospects and clients. They educate and inform in an indirect way that makes it seem as if they aren't trying to sell anything—quite the opposite. They want to give the impression that they just want the best for whomever they are talking to. This should be your whole attitude when talking to prospects.

Chapter 4: Making the Invitation

When it comes to actually inviting your prospects to be a part of your business, there are certain rules and principles that can really help you. This chapter will focus on how you can make a pitch or invitation that will give the best impression to your prospects and keep them interested. Having a great product or idea to pitch is half the battle; you also have to present it in such a way that it will highlight all the wonderful features of your product and the benefits your business offers. You have to be aware of subtle body language and words that could turn off potential prospects or clients as well as how to make your pitch more effective.

Factors to consider

Is it appropriate to do this here/now? This is the first thing you should ask yourself. Are the people you are about to pitch to willing to hear this? Is this an appropriate place or event to start selling your business idea or product? You can't just rush into talking about your business in every social situation. This can have a negative effect as people will only see you as the salesperson and may even end up avoiding you. Make sure you've read the room, or at least read their individual moods, before launching your pitch or inviting them to join your business.

How well do you know them? Are they warm-market prospects, or people who know and trust you, or are they cold-market prospects, or people you've just met and with whom you have only been briefly acquainted? This is important to note as marketing styles often vary between these two groups. For you to get the best out of it, you have to employ these different approaches skillfully.

What exactly do you want to get out of this right now? Is it a sale, is it an invitation, and if so, an invitation to what? A direct invitation to join the business, an event, or is it to make use of a tool? Do you want them to join your team, or do you just want to get acquainted for now? What you want to achieve in the end dictates how you handle the interaction with your prospect or client, so it's important that you have a clear idea of what your ends are.

A step by step guide to making an irresistible invitation:

Step 1: Act busy.

It has been proven that, psychologically, people are more attentive to someone who looks like they have a lot on their plate. Being in a hurry and giving your invitations and pitches an air of urgency will make people less resistant to what you have to say and so they will not want to waste your time.

You can start by saying: "I've been so busy, but I'm so glad I got to meet with you. This is really important," or "I really have somewhere to be right now, but I just had to talk to you really quickly." Choose your words accordingly; you don't have to follow the above examples exactly. Just focus on coming across as someone who's in a real hurry and remember to put some urgency in your voice.

Step 2: Don't be condescending; be approving.

There are a lot of marketers who commit a very basic mistake—being critical of new prospects. Because they want their new prospects to join them in their business, they tend to be critical of their prospect's life choices. This doesn't mean that they directly tell them that what they are doing is wrong, but there is a tendency of coming off as condescending. For example, do not reply with, "Really? You still work there?" in a tone of disbelief when your prospect tells you that they still work in a coffee shop.

Remember that your prospects will be much more inclined to share with you if you withhold the criticism. Instead, you could say, "Wow, it must be nice to still be working in the same company. How do you like it?" A reply like this will make your prospect more open to what you have to say and more willing to share whatever difficulties and dissatisfaction they may have.

Step 3: Present the actual invitation.

There are different ways that you can get your prospect to be interested in your product, or at least get them to look at it. There is a direct and an indirect approach. Of course, the direct approach can be best used for warm-market prospects or people whom you already know closely such as close friends and family members. However, if you choose your words carefully, you can get a lot of cold-market prospects as well. Use the direct approach to address a certain need in their lives. Following up on the example above, you can say, "Hey, if you're not so happy with your job, then maybe you're interested in starting a business without much risk?"

An indirect approach is more advisable for those who are just starting out and don't really have a reputation to begin with. This approach means you ask your prospects for help, guidance, or their expert input. This is a great way of complimenting them and, at the same time, informing and educating them about your business plans. This is an effective approach that you can use for prospects who have a lot of experience and are respected. This can be a potential gold mine as these prospects often have a lot of referrals that can add even more names to your client list.

Examples of the indirect approach would be the following:

"Hey, I've just started this business plan, and I really wanted to get your input about it, since you have a lot of experience in this. I'll make it really quick."

"I have this really great product that I wanted to put out there, but I'd really love to get an outsider's opinion on it. Would you mind if I explained it to you and asked you for your honest opinion about it?"

Chapter 5: About Tools, Events, and Getting Commitments

Once you've given them a basic run-down of your business, you can head on to using *Tools* or invite them to seminars and events hosted by the company. Remember that meeting your prospects once or twice will never be enough. It is a gradual process and you will have to keep inviting them to use or study more tools and go to more events.

Tools

Using tools is a great way to easily educate your prospect, as well making your business more legitimate in their eyes. A tool can be anything, from informational pamphlets, to DVDs, to the actual product that they can use to test out for themselves. These are very effective in getting your prospects to learn more about the product as well as allow them to see how they as end-users can benefit from it.

Events

Events are even more effective as they can help develop connections between your prospects and build up camaraderie. Through events, your prospects will be able to witness how big the organization actually is, and this can be a great boost in excitement and enthusiasm. But for those who are only starting out, organizing big events can be pretty difficult. You can suffer from getting very few turnouts, which can be discouraging.

The easiest ways that you can get commitments are using these tools and inviting prospects to the events the company holds, which are much more effective than just telling them about the products and benefits. Getting your marketing team to go to such events, even if these aren't "major" events, can help boost enthusiasm and drive.

Getting the commitment

It's time for you to get them to commit, and this is when you use the tools and events. You can either offer them the tool to use, study, and review, or you can invite them to an event. You need to get a commitment and a confirmation of the commitment.

Example: "So when are you going to read the pamphlet/watch the DVD/use the sample?" If your prospect replies that they will do it on Tuesday night, you can then say, "So if I called you on Wednesday morning, we'll definitely be able to talk about it then?" If they say yes, remember to confirm the next call.

Phrase this last confirmation this way: "So what time do you think I should call you?" or "When would be the best time for me to call and confirm?" The point here is that you ask THEM for the appointment; you are not the one giving it out. At this point, you've confirmed their commitment about 3 or 4 times, and the chances of them actually showing up or reviewing your product are greatly improved from when you first started.

Things to remember:

Be sincere. As mentioned before, you are not just selling to your clients and distributors; you are developing relationships with them. Being sincere in your praise, compliments, and well-wishes towards them will show, and this will make more and more people more enthusiastic about doing business with you.

Have empathy. This is an important aspect of strengthening your relationships with the team as well as with clients and distributors who are in need of guidance. Remember that arguing about it or putting them down will not solve anything—you have to look at it from their point of view and try to help. It is important that they feel understood, and with that, you can offer solutions that they will be able to find believable and thus make them more open to what you are offering.

Conclusion

Now that you've been treated to a rundown of steps and tips when it comes to making your pitch and presenting the business opportunity that you have to offer, you are better equipped to navigate the sea of network marketing. Remember that there will always be ups and downs in business, so don't let yourself get discouraged. Keep at it with sincerity and drive, and you will surely find success.

All that's left for you to do is to go out there and practice what you've learned. Have confidence in yourself and take the network marketing world by storm!

www.ingramcontent.com/pod-product-compliance
Lightning Source LLC
Chambersburg PA
CBHW050912180526
45159CB00007B/2889